Animals That SWIM

by Pearl Markovics

Consultant:
Beth Gambro
Reading Specialist
Yorkville, Illinois

Contents

BEARPORT
PUBLISHING

New York, New York

Animals That Swim

What can swim?

A fish can swim.

What can swim?

A seal can swim.

What can swim?

A bear can swim.

What can swim?

A hippo can swim.

What can swim?

A penguin can swim.

What can swim?

A dolphin can swim.

Can you swim?

Yes, you can!

Key Words

bear

dolphin

fish

hippo

penguin

seal

Index

About the Author

Pearl Markovics says that swimming is like riding a bike. Once you learn, you never forget!